THE BERLIN WALL

AN INTERACTIVE MODERN HISTORY ADVENTURE

by Matt Doeden

Consultant:
John DePerro, Curator
The Cold War Museum
Warrenton, Virginia

CAPSTONE PRESS
a capstone imprint

You Choose Books are published by Capstone Press,
1710 Roe Crest Drive, North Mankato, Minnesota 56003
www.capstonepub.com

Library of Congress Cataloging-in-Publication Data
Doeden, Matt.
  The Berlin Wall : an interactive modern history adventure / by Matt Doeden.
    pages cm. — (You choose. Modern history)
  Includes bibliographical references and index.
  Summary: "Lets readers experience life behind the Berlin wall, choosing different paths
to take through history"— Provided by publisher.
  Audience: Grades 4–6.
  ISBN 978-1-4914-0354-9 (library binding)
  ISBN 978-1-4914-0356-3 (paperback)
  ISBN 978-1-4914-0358-7 (eBook PDF)
1. Berlin Wall, Berlin, Germany, 1961-1989—Juvenile literature. 2. Berlin (Germany)—
History—1945-1990—Juvenile literature. 3. Germany—History—1945-1990—
Juvenile literature. 4. Cold War—Juvenile literature. 5. Plot-your-own stories. I. Title.
  DD881.D56 2015
  943'.1552087—dc23   2014013373

Editorial Credits
Mandy Robbins, editor; Bobbie Nuytten, designer; Wanda Winch, media researcher;
Charmaine Whitman, production specialist

Photo Credits
AP Images: DPA/Picture Alliance, 26, Lionel Cironneau, 101; Capstone, 9; Getty
Images: Express/Archive Photos, 66, Cleland Rimmer, 70, Express Newspaper, 41,
Gamma-Rapho/Dominique Berretty, 58, Keystone, 63, Popperfoto, 12, 38, Time Life
Pictures/Paul Schutzer, 48, 61, Tom Stoddart, cover, UIG/Sovfoto, 53; Landov: DPA,
21, 44, 75, 102, DPA/GIEHR, 14, Reuters, 83; Newscom: akg-images, 32, akg-images/
Gert Schuetz, 6, Reuters/David Baruchli, 91; Shutterstock: Valentin Agapov, wall
texture design element; SuperStock: imagebroker.net, 78, 89, 94

Printed and bound in China.
010729R

TABLE OF CONTENTS

4

ABOUT YOUR
ADVENTURE

YOU are living during the time of the Berlin Wall. Your city, Berlin, and your country, Germany, have been split in half. A Communist government rules East Germany, where you live. People there struggle with lack of money and resources. Many wish to cross to West Berlin to enjoy its freedom and wealth. What choices will you make as you face life in troubled East Berlin?

Chapter One sets the scene. You choose which path to read. Follow the directions at the bottom of each page. The choices you make will change your outcome. After you finish one path, go back and read the others for more adventures.

YOU CHOOSE the path
you take through history.

The Berlin Wall separated the residents of East Berlin from West Berlin.

CHAPTER 1

A Divided Germany

After World War II (1939–1945), Germany was a nation filled with conflict. The country had been part of a group of nations called the Axis powers. Germany joined Japan, Italy, and other Axis nations to fight the Allied forces. These included the United States, France, Great Britain, and the Soviet Union, which was made up of present-day Russia and several other countries.

The Allies won the war in 1945 and took over Germany. By 1949 Germany was split into two halves, the Federal Republic of Germany, known as West Germany, and the German Democratic Republic, known as East Germany.

Turn the page.

The city of Berlin was also split in two. It was located in East Germany, but its western half was considered part of West Germany. The United States gave $2.6 million and other aid that helped West Germany rebuild.

Life was more difficult in East Berlin and the rest of East Germany. The Soviet Union ruled there. They supplied no financial aid and had a Communist government. Under this system the government owned most property and businesses. Many East German leaders cared more about holding power than helping people. East Germany was left with little money and few resources to rebuild. Day-to-day life was a struggle.

During the war the United States and the Soviet Union had been allies. But the two powers grew more distrustful after the war. This distrust resulted in what was called the Cold War.

The wall cut the city of Berlin in half. Families and friends were separated. Workers were cut off from their jobs on the other side. The United States didn't try to stop the wall. Kennedy said privately, "a wall is … better than a war."

Historians believe more than 5,000 East Germans tried to escape. Guards were ordered to shoot anyone trying to cross into West Berlin. But many still tried. Some made it. Others died or were imprisoned. Best estimates put the number of people killed fleeing to the West at 1,065.

The Berlin Wall stood for 28 years. How will you experience this troubled time?

To witness the first days of the Berlin Wall as an East German teenager, turn to page **13**.

To serve as an East German guard on the Berlin Wall during the 1960s, turn to page **49**.

To experience the fall of the Berlin Wall in 1989, turn to page **79**.

Workers reinforce the Berlin Wall with cement blocks.

CHAPTER 2

To Stay or to Go

You hold your head in your hands. "What are we going to do?" you ask your older sister, Greta. Ever since your parents died, you and Greta have watched out for each other. Now you're facing one of the biggest decisions of your lives.

It is August 15, 1961, and your world has just been turned upside down. You and Greta live in East Berlin, but you travel each day into West Berlin to work in your uncle Arno's clothing shop. Many of your friends and cousins live in the West. Until today you've been able to visit them whenever you wished. But this morning all of that changed. No one is allowed to leave East Germany. Your job and way of life have been cut off.

13

Turn the page.

Your friend Peter stomps across the kitchen of your small East Berlin home. "Don't worry," he says. "The Americans won't stand for this. President Kennedy will have that wall down in no time."

"I'm not sure," Greta says. "The United States and the Soviet Union have been close to war for years. This wall solves problems for the Americans as well. It could be there for good."

Construction of the Berlin Wall begins on August 13, 1961.

"Nonsense," Peter scoffs. "Just wait. Be patient. Everything will be back to normal soon."

"That wall is only going to get bigger," Greta says. "If we're going to try to escape, we need to do it now."

"They're shooting anyone who tries!" Peter replies. "Why risk your lives?"

Greta slumps into a chair. You can tell she wants to escape. But she won't try it without you.

To agree with Greta and plan an escape into West Berlin, turn to page **16**.

To agree with Peter and wait, turn to page **17**.

"Greta is right. If we're going to go, we have to do it now."

Greta springs to her feet. "Pack your things. We'll go tonight."

"Hold on," Peter says. "If you're going to do this, do it right. Let's speak to my father. He'll help us come up with a plan."

You know Peter's father, Stefan Schultz, and trust him. He hates the Communists and what they've done to his country. But he's a careful man. He has money and knows people in power. His contacts might help you. But a delay could be the difference between success and failure.

"You know how I feel," Greta says. "The sooner we're in West Berlin, the better."

To agree to meet with Peter's father, turn to page **20**.

To plan an immediate escape, turn to page **23**.

You take Greta's hand. "Peter is right. We don't know anything. The wall could be down tomorrow, or in a week. And spies are everywhere. If we're caught trying to escape, we'll be captured or even killed."

And so you wait. Over the next several weeks, you watch as the wall grows. Concrete barriers go up behind coils of barbed wire. More and more border guards stand at the three checkpoints along the wall. Certain people can come and go through these checkpoints. But they need official papers, and there's no way you can get them. You and Greta search for work, but there's little to be had in the East. Food is growing scarcer. You wonder whether you've made a mistake.

17

Turn the page.

A few weeks later, you, Greta, and Peter walk along the wall. "There," Peter says, pointing to a place where guards are repairing a section of barbed wire near a checkpoint. "I saw it myself. Someone rammed the gate with a car. The guards fired at it, but it got through. We all cheered as the West Germans helped two young guys out of the car. They made it!"

"You said trying to escape was foolish, Peter."

"I was wrong. The Americans aren't going to help us. Come with me. I want you to meet Eva, a friend of my father's."

Peter leads you into the back room of a deserted store. A young woman greets you.

"Eva knows a man in West Germany who is digging a tunnel under the wall," Peter explains.

"Join us," Eva says. "My friend Wolfgang Fuchs will get us out. We have to wait. It may take months or even years. But what safer way could there be to escape than under the wall?"

Greta nods. But you're not sure. Peter says Fuchs is an optician. What does he know about building tunnels? What if the tunnel collapses? Do you trust this stranger with your life?

To agree to Eva's plan, turn to page **25**.

To tell Greta that it's too risky, turn to page **40**.

The next morning you and Greta go to Peter's house. Peter's family lives in a building near the wall. As you walk you take in the scene. Big coils of razor-sharp barbed wire form most of the wall. In some places workers are building large concrete barriers.

"They are moving fast," Greta says. You can tell she regrets waiting even one more day.

Peter and his father greet you at the door.

"Peter tells me the two of you plan to escape," his father, Herr Schultz, says. "Is that wise?"

20   "Staying here doesn't seem wise," Greta answers. "Things keep getting worse. And if we don't move now, the chance will be gone."

"I've given this some thought," Herr Schultz says. "I will help you, but you must take Peter with you."

East Berlin policemen guard the streets as construction crews begin building the Berlin Wall behind them.

Turn the page.

Peter starts to protest. But his father gives him a look that stops him. "Greta is right," Herr Schultz says. "Things will get worse. The West will thrive while the East suffers. Get out now."

"How?" you ask.

"I have two ideas. First, I own a building along the wall. You could climb to the third story and jump to safety. Or if you don't like the idea of jumping, there's another option. I've heard of a West German named Wolfgang Fuchs who is digging a tunnel. If you wait, I can get you in the group that he'll lead to freedom. My friend Eva is part of the group."

To try escaping through a tunnel, turn to page **25**.

To try jumping from a building along the wall, turn to page **27**.

You grab Peter's arm. "We should do it now, Peter. If the rumors are true, several people have already gotten away. It won't take the guards long to cut off all the easy ways to escape."

Peter again tries to talk you out of your plan, but you won't change your mind. Finally, he gives up. "I'm staying," he says. "This is a mistake. But I hope you both make it through all right. I'll visit you as soon as they take the wall down."

As the sun sets that evening, you and Greta prepare to move. You've narrowed your choices to two. You could find a remote section of the wall, cut through the barbed wire, and sneak across into West Berlin. Or you could approach one of the small, lightly guarded checkpoints, attack the guards, and rush through the gate before anyone else can respond.

23

Turn the page.

"I think we should cut our way through," Greta says. "Attacking armed guards seems a lot more dangerous."

"That's why it could work," you argue. "They won't expect it. We'll be through before anyone notices."

"It's up to you," Greta says. "I just want to get out tonight."

To try to cut through the barbed wire, turn to page **29**.

To attack the guards at a checkpoint, turn to page **30**.

Eva explains the plan. It's simple. Wolfgang and a team of West Germans are planning to dig several tunnels. He will come through and lead you back into the West.

"Be patient," Eva tells you. "This is going to take some time. All you need to do is stay quiet and wait."

So that's what you do. Weeks turn into months. Months turn into years. You work odd jobs to earn money and rely on friends for food when you don't have any. One day you're walking near the wall, gazing over to the other side. You bump into a childhood friend, Hans. Your conversation soon turns to the wall. "I've taken a real interest in the wall," Hans says. "I make it a point to learn all I can about escape attempts."

Turn the page.

Should you invite Hans to join your group? He sounds interested. You doubt Eva would mind. But you haven't seen Hans in years, and spies are everywhere. Can you trust him with your secret?

To keep quiet about the tunnel, turn to page **43**.

To invite Hans to join the group, turn to page **47**.

A woman successfully escapes East Berlin through a tunnel in 1964.

As crazy as it sounds, jumping over the wall seems like one of the safest choices you can make.

"It's settled," says Herr Schultz. "Go today. I've heard the government is boarding up windows in buildings along the wall. My building hasn't been touched yet. But it could happen at any time."

You and Greta step out as Peter says good-bye to his father. You're shaking as you approach the building. But no guards stand in your way. The building is mostly abandoned. You climb a narrow stairwell to the third floor. Peter uses a key to open the door of a small office with a window.

27

Turn the page.

You throw open the window and peer outside. It's late afternoon. Crowds of West German protesters line the streets below. Several spot you and point. Within minutes a group of West Germans has set up a net below the building. They're going to catch you!

"Footsteps!" Peter shouts. You hear them coming down the hall. Guards!

"Go!" Greta shouts. Peter is the first out. Your stomach churns as you watch him fall into the net. Suddenly you're not so sure you can do this. What if the protesters don't catch you?

To jump, turn to page **35**.

To hide in the shadows and try to find a safer escape later, turn to page **36**.

The two of you creep through the dark streets of East Berlin. Tall buildings stand alongside parts of the wall. You keep to their dark shadows as you approach.

The section of the wall ahead of you stands between two buildings. At the moment this section is only heavy, coiled barbed wire. Greta gets a wire cutter from her bag and cuts while you stand watch.

Moments later you see movement in the distance. "Hush!" you whisper. You both freeze. Voices approach. You're certain it's guards. If you're caught, you'll be imprisoned or shot. You look back at Greta. She's cut a hole in the fence. If you're going to go for it, now is the time.

To charge through the fence, turn to page **33**.

To stay hidden and hope the guards don't notice you, turn to page **36**.

Gated checkpoints are spread along the wall. You and Greta head toward a little-used checkpoint with hopes it will be lightly guarded.

You watch from the shadows. Two guards man the checkpoint. There's little traffic here. If your plan is going to work, this is the spot. You wait until one of the guards disappears into a small building. "I'll bet he's using the restroom," you tell Greta. "This is our best chance."

The remaining guard meets you as you approach. "Stop," he barks. "State your business."

"We need to pass," you reply, trying to sound confident. "Here, I have my papers."

The guard takes a step closer. You spring into action. You drive your knee up into his stomach. The guard grunts and doubles over. "Run!" you tell Greta.

The two of you charge the gate. But it's closed, and you fumble with the latch. As you throw it open, a gunshot rings through the night.

A voice shouts out. "On the ground! Now!" It's the other guard. Would he really shoot? All you have to do is sprint through the checkpoint into West Germany. Would your sudden action surprise him and give you time? Or is that a sure way to get killed?

To surrender, turn to page **37**.

To try to dash to safety, turn to page **39**.

32

East German guards catch
residents trying to flee East Berlin.

There's no more time. You've got to go. "Come on!" you whisper.

The hole Greta cut isn't large. You feel the barbs tearing through your skin as you crawl through. But you don't slow down. You'll get a lot worse than torn skin if the guards get to you.

Finally, you're through. You grab Greta's hand and help pull her through. You're both breathing hard and bleeding, but you don't stop. You're through the fence. You dart across an open courtyard, expecting bullets to fly in your direction at any moment. But no shots ring out. You made it!

33

Turn the page.

The two of you continue to your Uncle Arno's house, grateful to have survived. Two days later you return to the spot where you escaped. Sure enough, a tall concrete barrier now stands there. If you'd waited, you would never have had the chance to escape this way. You wish that Peter had come with you. It may be a long time until you see him again.

THE END

To follow another path, turn to page 11.
To read the conclusion, turn to page 103.

You step onto the open window and launch yourself away from the building. The fall takes only a second or two, but it feels like forever. Then you feel yourself slam into the net. You hit it at an awkward angle and feel a bone snap in your leg. The flash of pain is sharp as two West German teenagers help you to the ground.

You ignore the pain as you watch Greta jump from the window and land in the net. A big cheer goes up from the West German crowd as the three of you are helped away from the wall.

"We'll get you to a doctor," says one of the teenagers. You lean on him for support.

You're in a lot of pain, but you can't wipe the smile off of your face. A broken leg is a small price to pay for your freedom.

THE END

To follow another path, turn to page 11.
To read the conclusion, turn to page 103.

You freeze, hiding in the shadows and hoping that the guards don't notice you. But you have no such luck. "You there!" shouts one of the guards. "Stop where you are!"

Your heart sinks as the two guards grab you and lead you away. Greta is sobbing. You're not sure if she's crying about missing her opportunity for freedom or because of the prospect of being thrown into prison.

It could be worse. You didn't escape, but at least you're still alive. Maybe you'll get another chance someday.

THE END

To follow another path, turn to page 11.
To read the conclusion, turn to page 103.

Your lives aren't worth the risk. You put your hands into the air and drop to your knees. Greta does the same. "I'm sorry," you whisper as the guards roughly grab you.

"I wish you'd run," says the guard you attacked with a snarl. "You are worth a month's pay, dead." Guards who killed those trying to flee received a cash reward.

You and Greta were just a few steps from freedom, but now you're almost certainly headed to a prison cell.

THE END

To follow another path, turn to page 11.
To read the conclusion, turn to page 103.

East German soldiers stand guard on the Berlin Wall in 1961.

38

"Run!" you shout, charging through the gate. A shot rings out, but you don't feel anything. The guard must have missed!

You're almost to freedom when you realize that you no longer hear Greta running behind you. She's on the ground, facedown, with blood staining her green coat. The sight brings you to a stop. The guard didn't miss. He shot Greta!

You know you should run. You might still make it. Greta would want you to get to safety. But the sight of your sister lying there, bleeding, freezes you in your tracks. Moments later, you see the flash of another gunshot. It's the last thing you ever see.

39

THE END

To follow another path, turn to page 11.
To read the conclusion, turn to page 103.

"I'm sorry," you say. "This just doesn't feel right to me. I don't want any part of it."

"What are you doing?" cries Greta. "This is our chance!"

"It's too risky."

"You think everything is too risky! Do you even want to escape?"

Greta storms off into the city. You hope her anger will pass, but the two of you speak little over the next few weeks. Every time you try to reason with her, you end up arguing. Then one day Greta is gone. Without telling you, she joined a group that rammed a car through a checkpoint.

40

Turn the page.

An escapee drops into the back
of a truck after scaling the Berlin
Wall with a ladder.

B·DM 441

You're glad she got what she wanted. But you miss her. In the years that follow, you often think of your choices in those early days of the Berlin Wall. Greta was right. Any escape attempt came with a risk that you weren't willing to take. Now the wall is bigger. A 110-yard open space called the Death Strip stands behind concrete barriers, where it's almost impossible to escape the guards' bullets. You missed your chance. Now you're trapped in East Berlin, away from your family.

"One day the wall may come down," you whisper to yourself. "All I can do is wait."

THE END

To follow another path, turn to page 11.
To read the conclusion, turn to page 103.

You can't risk trusting Hans. "Yes," you say, pretending not to be interested. "Some people are crazy, risking their lives to get over a wall."

Hans gives you a long, hard look. After a moment, he shakes your hand. "Nice to see you again. Say hello to your sister for me."

You take a deep breath, and then return home. You almost blew the secret. You're not sure how much longer you can stand to wait.

But the wait isn't forever. In early October 1964, Greta comes home with news. "I just spoke to Eva. The tunnel is complete! We meet tonight, after sunset. We're going to get out of here!"

43

Turn the page.

This escape tunnel ended in the basement of a West Berlin home.

44

At daybreak, you, Greta, Peter, and a handful of other young East Germans gather at an apartment on Sterlitzer Street. You arrive one or two at a time so that you don't attract attention. Every moment you half expect the border guards to crash in and arrest everyone. But it doesn't happen.

The tunnel's entrance is in the apartment's bathroom floor. As promised, Wolfgang leads the group through the 475-foot tunnel. Your heart races as you crawl silently through the dark, narrow space. All you hear is the rapid breathing of Greta and the others with you. You're sure that at any moment, the tunnel will collapse around you. Or that guards will storm in from behind you, shooting.

Turn the page.

But none of that happens. You see a light up ahead. Within moments, you're back above ground. "We're free!" Greta cries, rushing up to give Wolfgang a hug.

"Now go," Wolfgang says. "But tell no one of the tunnel, or of how you escaped. There will be more."

"Come on," Greta says, taking your hand. "Let's go to Uncle Arno's house and see the rest of our family."

THE END

To follow another path, turn to page 11.
To read the conclusion, turn to page 103.

"You're interested in escape?" you ask Hans. "Then I have something to tell you."

The two of you walk along the wall. "There's a man in West Berlin who is digging a tunnel. My friends and I are going to escape under the wall."

Hans clears his throat. "Tell me more. Who is planning this? Where is the tunnel?"

"Come with me, I'll show—"

You stop in the middle of your sentence. Two border guards are walking toward you. One nods. "You working tonight, Hans?" he asks.

Too late, you realize Hans is a border guard! You turn to run, but Hans grabs you by the arm.

"You have some explaining to do," he says, dragging you away.

THE END

To follow another path, turn to page 11.
To read the conclusion, turn to page 103.

An East German guard mans
the gate at a checkpoint.

CHAPTER 3

Guarding the Wall

You stand atop a guard tower on the Berlin Wall. As a member of the German Democratic Republic (GDR) border guard, you can see both sides of the divided city.

A crowd gathers on the west side of the wall. The West Germans shout at you, "Traitor!" But you ignore them. West Germans have protested the wall since it was built a few months ago. They don't know how difficult life is in East Berlin.

49

You chose to become a "Stasi," a member of the secret police. By doing so you're better off than other East Germans. You are paid twice that of an average worker. You have food, shelter, and money. There are far worse fates. Besides, it's almost sundown. The protesters will leave soon.

Turn the page.

Captain Bauer stands at your side. "I need you to pick up an extra shift," he says. "A few men are out sick."

"Sure, I can do that," you say. You don't feel like working another shift, but you know this is really more of an order than a request.

"Hmm," the captain says, glancing at a roster. "Do you want checkpoint duty or patrol duty?"

Normally you prefer patrol duty. You enjoy walking along the wall, making sure nobody is trying to escape. But after a long shift, checkpoint duty would be easier. All you have to do is check the papers of anyone wishing to pass into or out of East Berlin. It's dull, but easier on your feet.

To take checkpoint duty, go to page **51**.

To take patrol duty, turn to page **55**.

50

You take your post at Checkpoint C, which westerners call Checkpoint Charlie. It's the only checkpoint along the wall that allows entry to Americans and other members of the Allied forces. You, along with several other guards, must keep the gate secure. No one can get in or out without approval. You wear a white belt and hat, along with white arm covers. The white equipment is meant to make you more visible to motorists passing through the checkpoint.

"I heard there was an escape attempt earlier tonight," another guard, Thomas, tells you. "Two kids tried to cut through the fence. One of them even made it!"

"What about the other?" you ask.

Turn the page.

Thomas points his finger like a gun, closing his thumb as though pulling the trigger. "You know our orders."

You find the news depressing. So many people have died trying to escape.

The noise of an approaching vehicle interrupts your thoughts. Thomas stands to speak with the driver. You stand back, watching carefully. Thomas and the driver are speaking angrily at one another. You step up. "What's the problem?"

"Americans," Thomas says with a sneer. "They think they can just come and go whenever they please."

A few West Berliners were allowed to pass through a checkpoint to visit relatives in 1963.

Turn the page.

The vehicle carries an American diplomat. Diplomats are supposed to be allowed into and out of East Germany. But for some reason, Thomas doesn't like this one. Thomas is older than you and has worked longer as a guard. You're not sure you want to challenge him.

To disagree with Thomas and let the diplomat through, turn to page **57**.

To deny the diplomat entry, turn to page **76**.

You agree to take patrol duty. But you won't be alone. You'll be working with one of your unit's dogs, a German shepherd named Max. Max's keen sense of smell has located attempted escapees in the past. You're glad for the company.

You and Max move slowly along the wall. You keep your eyes peeled for anything suspicious. You look for any damage to the wall or other unusual activity.

As you walk you notice a group of East Berlin teens gathered near the wall. They're speaking to each other in hushed tones. They haven't seen you yet. You stop short, with Max at your side.

Turn the page.

"What's this?" you whisper to Max. You don't know whether they're up to anything. They could just be talking. But something feels strange about the gathering.

To observe the group, turn to page **59**.

To ignore them and continue on your patrol, turn to page **61**.

You grab Thomas by the shoulder and lead him away. "We can't do this," you say. "He has his papers. We'll get in trouble if we don't let him in."

Thomas shrugs. "Fine, let him in." He stomps off as you return to the vehicle.

"Sorry about that," you say, inspecting the diplomat's papers. "Go on through."

All is quiet until just before the end of your shift. That's when you hear the roar of an engine on the East German side of the wall. Suddenly, a shout goes up from a nearby tower. "Truck!"

You turn and see a truck coming fast straight at the gate. They're going to ram it! You have to act fast.

To block the gate, turn to page 65.

To get out of the way, turn to page 67.

58

East Berlin policemen inspect a sewer
drain for escapees near the wall.

You order Max to stay as you creep in closer to the group of kids. You stay in the shadows along the side of a building. From that position, you're able to pick out words and phrases.

" … Cut through the wire … before the guards spot us …"

They're planning an escape! You step out of the shadows and shout, "Stop right there!"

The teenagers freeze as they see you. Max approaches at the sound of your voice. The kids know better than to run.

A girl steps forward. "Is that you? It's me—Verda!" It takes you a second before you realize who is speaking to you. It's Verda, a girl from your neighborhood. Her brother Fritz used to be your best friend. What are you supposed to do now?

Turn the page.

She sees the expression on your face. "You don't have to do this. Just walk away. You never saw us or heard anything."

"I can't. It's my job. I have to bring you in."

"Then join us. We have a plan. Fritz is over there. Come with us!" She steps forward and takes your hand. Your heart is racing.

To join Verda and her friends in their escape attempt, turn to page **68**.

To arrest them, turn to page **71**.

"I don't see anything wrong here," you tell Max, scratching his head. "Let's keep moving."

You move on along the wall, noticing a tall building. During the early days of the wall, people jumped out of windows near the wall to reach West Berlin. But now all of the windows on the lower floors are sealed off with brick.

A young man attempts to escape over the Berlin Wall.

Turn the page.

The sound of gunfire cuts off your thought. You and Max run back the way you came. "Escape attempt!" shouts a fellow guard in one of the towers above the wall.

You rush to help, but it's too late. By the time you reach the site, the escapees are already safely in West Berlin. Captain Bauer calls you into his office. "Four teenagers escaped, right under our noses. How did that happen?" He doesn't know you actually saw the escapees before they left. But they got away on your watch. You know it's not a mark in your favor.

62   Over the next few months, you do your job without incident. But you don't forget your failure with the escapees.

Turn to page 64.

An East Berlin woman drops from a window into West Berlin.

63

One afternoon in August 1962, you're manning one of the guard towers near Checkpoint Charlie. You notice movement below in the Death Strip, the 110-yard open area that now stands between the concrete barriers. Two people are trying to dash across! This is your chance to redeem yourself.

To shoot at them, turn to page **72**.

To call for help, turn to page **74**.

Your job is to guard the gate, and that's what you'll do. You stand and turn to the truck, your rifle in your hands. Surely they see you and won't ram into you!

You raise your rifle, ready to fire. But the truck doesn't slow down. In fact, it's speeding up! Too late you realize that there's nothing you can do to stop it. You try to dive out of the way. But the truck clips you and sends you flying. You hear bones crunching as you slam into the gate. You black out.

You wake up a few days later in a hospital bed. You look down to see both of your legs missing. "We couldn't save them," a nurse explains. "The car crushed your legs. The doctors had to amputate each above the knee."

65

Turn the page.

You're going to live. But you'll never walk again, and your time as a member of the Stasi is over. What will happen to you now?

An East Berlin driver removed the windshield from his car so he could drive under a gate into West Berlin.

THE END

To follow another path, turn to page 11.
To read the conclusion, turn to page 103.

Your job is to guard the gate, not to get killed by a speeding truck! You jump out of the way and watch the truck crash through the gate. Guards on nearby towers open fire. Bullets tear through the truck's body and windshield. You shiver, knowing that the people inside must be dead.

Captain Bauer calls you into his office at the end of your shift. "I'm sorry," you say. "The truck wasn't going to stop. I had to get out of the way."

"Don't worry, you're not in trouble," he says. "I heard about what happened with that American diplomat. Thank you for stepping in. If we had denied him entry, there would have been a huge mess." He claps you on the back. "Take the weekend off. When you come back, there will be a promotion waiting for you."

THE END

To follow another path, turn to page 11.
To read the conclusion, turn to page 103.

This is a chance to escape your dreary life. "Yes, I'll do it," you say. Verda smiles and hugs you. "But we have to go now. Another guard will be by any minute."

You give Max one last pat on the head and order him to stay.

"Let's go!" says Verda. The group of you approach a section of barbed wire. Two of the young men begin to cut through as others stand watch. Your heart is racing. How long do you have?

Within minutes, you're through. But you still need to get over the concrete wall. One man throws a weighted rope over the wall. He's up and over in a flash. Two more join him before you're spotted. A gunshot rings out. There's not going to be enough time!

"Go!" you shout, pulling out your rifle. You shoot back, away from the guard tower, but close enough to make any guards more cautious. In a few seconds, you're the only one left. You grab the rope and pull yourself up. Another shot rings out. You feel pain jolt up your leg. You've been shot!

Before you lose your grasp, Another escapee grabs you by the shoulders. He pulls you up and over the barrier. He and another young man help you make the final run to freedom.

"It doesn't look too bad," Verda says, looking at your wound. "But we need to get a doctor."

69

"He needs a change of clothes too," another man says. "That uniform isn't going to make you very popular on this side of the wall."

THE END

To follow another path, turn to page 11.
To read the conclusion, turn to page 103.

Guards from East and West Berlin face each other over the Wall.

70

This is your job. You can't just let them go, and you're not going to risk your own life to get over the wall.

"I'm sorry, Verda," you say. As you call for help, two members of the group flee back into East Berlin. There's no need to chase them, and you don't want to send Max from your side. You're sure the East German police will get their names from those you do capture.

More guards arrive within minutes. You watch with some regret as they lead Verda away. Captain Bauer pats your back. "Well done. I can tell you have a bright future helping us defend our border."

71

THE END

To follow another path, turn to page 11.
To read the conclusion, turn to page 103.

You can't afford to let more people escape on your watch. It would probably cost you your job. You shout, "Stop or I'll shoot!" But the two men don't stop. You raise your rifle, aim, and fire. Crack! The gunshot echoes off the brick buildings, along with shots from other guards nearby. One of the escapees makes it through the bullets to the other side. But the other crumples to the ground, only a few dozen feet from the other side.

The young man lies on the ground. He's not dead, but he can't move. On the other side of the wall stand West Germans, as well as American military police. But none of them dare step into the Death Strip to help, knowing they could be shot.

Later you learn the man's name, Peter Fechter. He is only 18 years old. You can do nothing as Fechter lies there, slowly dying as he screams for help. About an hour later, Fechter dies. You watch as a group of East German guards carries him away.

You did your job. Your orders were to shoot. But you know that the image of Fechter lying there dying will never leave you.

THE END

To follow another path, turn to page 11.
To read the conclusion, turn to page 103.

"Escapees!" you shout, laying your rifle down beside you.

Guards arrive at the scene. Several fire, and one of the men crumples to the ground. But the other man escapes.

"What happened?" shouts the captain. "Your orders were to fire! Why didn't you shoot?"

"I ... I don't know," you answer.

The captain shakes his head. "You know what I have to do. Some men are not cut out for this job. Gather your things."

74

You don't argue. He's right. You're not sure how you'll find another job and earn a living. But one thing is certain. Your time guarding the Berlin Wall is over.

THE END

To follow another path, turn to page 11.
To read the conclusion, turn to page 103.

East Berlin police build a watchtower in a cemetery next to the Berlin Wall.

You don't want to go against your fellow guard. You stand by Thomas with your fingers resting on your rifle. "I'm sorry. Your papers aren't in order," you lie. "You'll have to turn around."

After a few more minutes of argument, the diplomat finally gives up. Thomas grins. "Americans. They think they can go anywhere and do whatever they want. Ha!"

But it doesn't seem so funny a few days later. A group of 10 American tanks lines up along the West German side of the wall. Then a group of 10 Soviet tanks follows. It's a standoff, and it's all happening because you refused to let the American diplomat cross.

The standoff continues for 16 hours. Neither side is willing to open fire. Then one Soviet tank backs down, followed by an American tank. One by one, the tanks leave. No shots are fired, so no harm is done. But the incident gets the world's attention. The Cold War is stronger than ever. You wonder if it will lead to a real war one day.

THE END

To follow another path, turn to page 11.
To read the conclusion, turn to page 103.

Residents of Berlin chisel out chunks of the Wall.

CHAPTER 4

The Last Days

You can hear the chant from your small East German apartment. "Wir sind das Volk! Wir sind das Volk!" It means, "We are the people! We are the people!" The protesters in the town square below are shouting it as loudly as they can.

You glance at your desk calendar. It reads November 4, 1989. Not long ago no one would have dared such a public protest. But over the past year, things have been changing. Several nearby countries have voted out their Communist governments. The Soviet Union is allowing its people more and more freedom. And an increasing number of East Germans are demanding that the Berlin Wall be torn down.

79

Turn the page.

Your older brother, Karl, is putting on his boots. "Let's join them. Just listen to that chant. Change is coming. Can't you feel it?"

You want freedom as badly as anyone. But all your life, you've learned to keep your anti-Communist thoughts to yourself. And only a few weeks ago, thousands of protesters were beaten and arrested by police. Is it worth risking your safety just to join in a protest?

To go with Karl and join the protest, go to page **81**.

To stay home, turn to page **84**.

You step into Alexanderplatz, East Berlin's main square. People surround you. Young and old, they have gathered to demand change. Some want freedom, democracy, and to be reunited with West Germany. Others are calling for a reformed government that offers its people more freedom. Today they are united in protest. And they all seem to agree that it's time for the Berlin Wall to come down.

As you stand and listen to speakers calling for change, you notice a small group of young men approaching a group of police.

"What are you doing?" you ask one of the men in the group.

Turn the page.

"See those police?" he asks, pointing. "They're under orders not to respond to us with violence. That means we can finally tell them what we think of them!"

"Is that wise?" Karl asks. "Why take the risk?"

The young men appear to be having a good time. They're laughing and shouting insults. So far the police haven't responded. What should you do?

To join their protest, turn to page **86**.

To stay with the peaceful rally, turn to page **87**.

East German riot police run through the streets during a protest in 1989.

83

"I think I'll stay here," you say. "You never know when the police will crack down on something like that."

Karl shrugs his shoulders and heads out the door. You lean out of your window, listening to the people in the nearby city square. You can hardly believe they're so willing to protest like this in public. No, that kind of risk isn't for you.

You stay close to home for the next few days. Karl is sure something big is about to change. "Other countries are opening their borders," he says. "Poland, Hungary. I think East Germany is going to be next."

He's out protesting again November 9. That evening you hear the roar of a crowd outside. People are cheering. You lean out the window to see what's happening.

Dozens of people are streaming past. They're all headed toward the wall. One young woman notices you. "What are you doing up there?" she asks with a smile. "Haven't you heard? They've opened the border! We can go into West Germany now!"

Could it be true? The border has been closed your entire life. If the wall were really open, it would be an historic occasion. You wouldn't want to miss it. But what if the woman is wrong and the border guards still have orders to shoot anyone who tries to escape?

85

To check it out, turn to page **89**.

To wait until tomorrow, turn to page **94**.

"He's right," you tell Karl. "The police have orders not to resort to violence. Let's tell them what we think of them!"

You join the others shouting insults at the police. The police ignore you. Then someone begins throwing things at them.

"They're throwing coins," Karl says, tugging your arm. "Just like the protesters did last month when they marched on the Parliament building. That didn't end well. Neither will this! We should get out of here."

To return to the peaceful rally, go to page **87**.

To throw coins at the police, turn to page **96**.

The Alexanderplatz protest stretches on. Actors, writers, and politicians speak to the crowd, demanding change. As you listen to speeches and join in the chants, you feel a sense of hope. You've lived your entire life trapped behind the Berlin Wall. This is the first time you've ever really believed things could change.

You hold onto that hope for the next several days. There is a new mood in East Berlin. For the first time in years, people are starting to believe change is possible. The evening of November 9, you and Karl are at home. You watch a press conference on TV, during which East German official Günter Schabowski gives a shocking announcement. He says that effective immediately, East Germans are free to travel to the West.

Turn the page.

You leap out of your seat. "Let's go!"

"Start without me," Karl says. "I want to tell some friends. I'll meet you at the checkpoint."

A large crowd moves toward a nearby checkpoint. Young and old are buzzing at the news that the border has opened. But when you reach the checkpoint, the gates remain closed.

"Let us through!" people shout to the guards. At first the guards don't seem to know what to do. One speaks to the crowd, ordering everyone to go to a nearby office to get official papers. But this only makes the crowd angry. You spot Karl and his friends among them. He greets you with a big smile.

The minutes tick by as you stand outside the gate. You're afraid that some people might try to rush through. The guards seem to share the same fear. One guard speaks frantically to the others. You inch closer so you can hear. "Open the barrier," he shouts. "Let them through!"

Excited Berliners from both sides of the Wall climb it as news spreads that it is coming down.

Turn the page.

Just like that, the Berlin Wall is open to all. Karl cheers as East Germans begin to pour through into West Berlin. But others move away from the gate. "Where are you going?" Karl asks.

"To tear down the wall!" a young man answers. "Come with us!"

To go through the gate to West Berlin, turn to page **92**.

To help tear down the wall, turn to page **98**.

A protester takes a sledgehammer to
the Berlin Wall on November 11, 1989.

"Thanks," you say with a wave. "But I've always wanted to see the other side of this wall. I'm not waiting another minute."

You and Karl join the stream of cheering people pouring into West Berlin. On the other side, thousands of West Berliners have gathered to greet you. You find yourself hugging complete strangers. The crowd grows throughout the night. You watch families reunited. You cheer as young men and women take chisels and hammers to the wall and tear it down, piece by piece. Before long there are so many people chipping away at it that the stores are completely out of chisels.

The celebration goes on through the night and into the following day. You cheer as West German chancellor Helmut Kohl speaks of a united Germany. But by noon you're too tired to keep celebrating. "Should we go home?" Karl asks.

You're not sure what to do. Now that you've seen West Berlin, you realize how run down the East is. Everything about the West is nicer and more modern. Do you really want to go back to your little apartment? Do you trust the East German government not to close the border again? On the other hand, the East has always been your home. If no one stays, how can it ever be rebuilt?

To return home to East Berlin, turn to page **99**.

To stay in West Berlin and make a new life, turn to page **100**.

You can't believe the government would allow you to cross into West Berlin. It sounds too good to be true. What if they change their minds? Would they arrest or shoot those trying to leave? It has to be safer to wait and see what happens.

A reporter at the Brandenburg Gate broadcasts the fall of the Berlin Wall.

The next day the city is buzzing. Thousands of people are literally tearing the wall apart. Many more have already flocked to West Berlin.

Not you, though. Maybe someday you'll cross into West Berlin. But now there are thousands of people over there. It must be mass confusion. You'll stay here for now. After all, if you never take a risk, you can never get hurt. So what if history is happening right outside your door?

THE END

To follow another path, turn to page 11.
To read the conclusion, turn to page 103.

"They're never going to hear our message if we stay quiet," you explain. You dig into your pockets and find a few coins. The first one you throw sails above the heads of the police. But the second hits one square in the arm.

Within moments, the police swarm in. An officer grabs your arm and drives a knee into your stomach. He forces you to the ground, slapping handcuffs on your wrists. The officer then takes you and Karl to the police station and puts you in a prison cell with dozens of other protesters.

That's where you spend the next several nights. And you're still there on the evening of November 9, when the East German government finally listens to its people. The Berlin Wall comes down. While thousands rush into the West to celebrate their first real taste of freedom, you and Karl are locked up in a dingy prison cell.

You'll get out of prison eventually. But you can't believe you missed such a big historical event. You'll scold yourself for a long time. And you're sure Karl will too.

THE END

To follow another path, turn to page 11.
To read the conclusion, turn to page 103.

"I've been looking at this ugly wall all my life," you say. "Let's tear it down!"

Karl lets out a whoop and the two of you join the crowd. Along the way someone hands you an old chisel. You hop up onto a concrete barrier and get to work. Within a few minutes, you've hacked off a fist-sized chunk of concrete. "I'm keeping this," you tell Karl, who takes the chisel and starts chipping at the wall. "I never want to forget this moment. I'm going to show this to my grandchildren one day and tell them about the night we tore down the Berlin Wall."

THE END

To follow another path, turn to page 11.
To read the conclusion, turn to page 103.

"The wall is down now," you say. "I don't think it will be going back up again. Let's go home. There will be a lot of work to do. Our friends and neighbors will need all the help they can get."

It feels strange crossing back into East Berlin. Large sections of the wall have already been torn down. People are carrying off chunks of it for souvenirs. You spot an East German border guard standing nearby, but he barely even looks in your direction. You wonder what will happen to him. What will happen to the entire government?

"One thing is for sure," Karl says. "We may be going back home, but life will never be the same."

99

THE END

To follow another path, turn to page 11.
To read the conclusion, turn to page 103.

"I've wanted to come here my whole life," you say. "I'm not going back. What if East Germany decides to close the border again? We'd never forgive ourselves."

The two of you cross the border, but only to collect your things. By evening your bags are packed, and you're headed back to West Berlin. What waits for you there? You don't know. But you're excited to start building a new life with freedom you've never before experienced.

THE END

To follow another path, turn to page 11.
To read the conclusion, turn to page 103.

East German border guards look through a section of the Berlin Wall as demonstrators pull it down.

A woman escapes her East Berlin apartment through a second-story window as police try to pull her back. The street below is part of West Berlin.

CHAPTER 5

Together Again

The Berlin Wall stood as a symbol of the conflict between the Soviet Union and the United States for 28 years. It marked a division of a city, a country, and a continent.

While the wall stood, people used many creative ways to attempt escape. They jumped from buildings. They rammed checkpoints with cars. One man escaped using a tightrope. Two families even escaped in a homemade hot air balloon in 1979. No one knows exactly how many people tried to escape, how many made it, and how many were caught or killed. Official records claimed 100 people died while trying to escape. But most historians believe that number is more than 1,000.

Change came fast in 1989. Poland removed the Communists from power in August. Hungary followed in October. East Germans demanded change. One Berlin protest in November drew at least 500,000 people. East German leaders had little choice. They opened the borders.

East German official Günter Schabowski mistakenly announced at a November 9 televised press conference that East Germans could leave immediately. That hadn't been the plan. The border was to have been opened the next day. But East Germans swarmed into West Berlin right away. East and West Berliners joined together to tear down large sections of the wall.

The East German Communist leaders were voted out of office in early 1990. East and West Germany reunited as one nation in October, with Berlin as its capital.

The Soviet empire was crumbling. One nation after the next declared independence. Finally, on December 8, 1991, the Soviet Union officially came to an end.

Meanwhile, Germans struggled to rebuild the East. The West was far more wealthy and modern. Some westerners resented the cost of updating the East. But a unified Germany has thrived in recent years. It remains an important part of the present-day European Union.

The Berlin Wall is gone, but not forgotten. Most of it was torn down in the days and weeks after the wall fell. Many tore down bits of the wall as souvenirs. But a few sections remain. They stand as a reminder of the dark days that followed World War II.

TIMELINE

1945—The Allied forces defeat Germany and the other Axis powers in World War II. The Allies divide Germany into four occupation zones.

1949—Germany is divided into two countries. The U.S., French, and British zones in the West become the Federal Republic of Germany. The Soviet zone in the East becomes the German Democratic Republic.

1950s—Millions of East Germans flee to West Germany in search of a better life.

1961

August 12—2,400 East Germans flee to West Berlin, the most to escape during one day.

August 13—East Germany begins building the Berlin Wall.

October 22—U.S. diplomat E. Allan Lightner is refused entry into East Berlin. A standoff between U.S. and Soviet tanks follows. No shots are fired and the crisis passes in less than a day.

1962—A second fence is built, leaving an open space of about 110 yards between. This space becomes known as the Death Strip.

1964—West German Wolfgang Fuchs builds Tunnel 57; through it he helps 57 East Germans escape.

1975—East Germany adds to the wall by building 12-foot concrete walls topped with pipes to prevent people from climbing them.

1987—On June 12 U.S. President Ronald Reagan makes a speech at the Brandenburg Gate near the Berlin Wall, telling Soviet leader Mikhail Gorbachev to "tear down this wall."

1989

September—Protests increase in East Germany. The most famous are the weekly Monday protests in the city of Leipzig.

October 7—Police attack and arrest protesters in East Berlin and several other East German cities.

November 4—Between 500,000 and 1 million people take part in the Alexanderplatz demonstration in East Berlin.

November 9—East German official Günter Schabowski announces during a televised press conference that the Berlin Wall is open. East Germans and West Germans begin tearing down the wall.

1990—East and West Germany unify October 3.

1991—The Soviet Union officially dissolves.

December 26, 2013—People protest as historical sections of the Berlin Wall are torn down to make room for new development.

OTHER PATHS
TO EXPLORE

In this book you've seen how the Berlin Wall affected lives in Germany from several different points of view. Perspectives on history are as varied as the people who lived it. Explore more paths on your own to learn more about the Berlin Wall.

People in West Berlin had more prosperity and freedom than those in East Berlin. But the wall still separated their city. How might have West German teens felt about the wall going up? Would they have been angry? Or afraid? (Common Core: Integration of Knowledge and Ideas)

U.S. President John F. Kennedy was at the center of the Berlin Wall controversy. How do you think he felt about the Soviet Union and East Germany building the wall? Would it have been worth going to war to stop it? Or did the wall offer Kennedy a solution to some of his problems as well? (Common Core: Key Ideas and Details)

Many East Germans celebrated when the wall fell. But how did East Germans loyal to the Communist Party feel about it? Would they have been sad at the failure of their government? Nervous about a return to capitalism? Or afraid for their safety because the unpopular Communist Party could no longer protect them? (Common Core: Integration of Knowledge and Ideas)

READ MORE

Burgan, Michael. *The Berlin Wall: Barrier to Freedom*. Minneapolis: Compass Point Books, 2008.

Colson, Mary. *Germany.* Chicago: Heinemann Library, 2012.

Harrison, Paul. *Why Did the Cold War Happen?* New York: Gareth Stevens Pub., 2011.

Hay, Jeff T., ed. *The Fall of the Berlin Wall*. Detroit: Greenhaven Press, 2010.

INTERNET SITES

Use FactHound to find Internet sites related to this book. All of the sites on FactHound have been researched by our staff.

Here's all you do:
Visit *www.facthound.com*
Type in this code: 9781491403549

GLOSSARY

amputate (AM-pyuh-tate)—to surgically cut off an arm or leg

atomic weapon (uh-TAH-mik WEP-uhn)—a weapon that uses nuclear power to create massive destruction

capitalism (KAP-uh-tuh-liz-uhm)—an economic system in which individuals and companies own most businesses and property

chancellor (CHAN-suh-luhr)—the head of the German government

checkpoint (CHEK-point)—a spot on a road or border where vehicles are stopped for inspection

communism (KAHM-yuh-ni-zuhm)—a form of government that limits personal freedom and the right to own property

democracy (di-MAH-kruh-see)—a form of government in which the people elect their leaders

diplomat (DIP-luh-mat)—someone who represents his or her government in another country

Herr (HARE)—the German word for "Mr."

optician (op-TISH-uhn)—someone who makes or sells eyeglasses

parliament (PAR-luh-muhnt)—a group of people who have been elected to make the laws in some countries

BIBLIOGRAPHY

Katona, Marianna S. *Tales from the Berlin Wall: Recollections of Frequent Crossings.* London: Minerva Press, 1997.

Kempe, Frederick. *Berlin 1961: Kennedy, Krushchev, and the Most Dangerous Place on Earth.* New York: G. P. Putnam's Sons, 2011.

Major, Patrick. *Behind the Berlin Wall: East Germany and the Frontiers of Power.* New York: Oxford University Press, 2010.

Rottman, Gordon L. *The Berlin Wall and the Intra-German Border, 1961–89.* Oxford: Osprey, 2008.

Schmemann, Serge. *When the Wall Came Down: The Berlin Wall and the Fall of Soviet Communism.* Boston: Kingfisher, 2006.

Schnibben, Cordt. *"The Guard Who Opened the Berlin Wall: 'I Gave my People the Order—Raise the Barrier.'"* Spiegel Online International. 9 Nov. 2009. 5 Feb. 2014. http://www.spiegel.de/international/germany/the-guard-who-opened-the-berlin-wall-i-gave-my-people-the-order-raise-the-barrier-a-660128.html

Taylor, Fred. *The Berlin Wall: A World Divided, 1961–1989.* New York: HarperCollins, 2006.

INDEX